IMAGES
of America

SNYDER AND
SCURRY COUNTY

IMAGES
of America

SNYDER AND
SCURRY COUNTY

Scurry County Museum

ARCADIA
PUBLISHING

Published by Arcadia Publishing
Charleston, South Carolina

Library of Congress Control Number: 2012950168

For all general information, please contact Arcadia Publishing:
Telephone 843-853-2070
Fax 843-853-0044
E-mail sales@arcadiapublishing.com
For customer service and orders:
Toll-Free 1-888-313-2665

Visit us on the Internet at www.arcadiapublishing.com

*The authors would like to thank Drew Bullard, Jerry
Corkran, and Norman Brown for all their help.*

CONTENTS

ACKNOWLEDGMENTS

The tireless efforts of our staff, volunteers, and student workers have all contributed to this book. Unless listed otherwise, all photographs are the property of the Scurry County Museum. We would also like to thank Baylor Athletics, the Associated Press, Getty Images (*Time and Life Magazine*), the US Army Signal Corps, and Monica Karales (*The Estate of James Karales*) for assisting us with additional photographs. We were not able to include everyone's photographs, but we appreciate the fact that so many people were willing to help.

INTRODUCTION

West Texas has always been a blue-collar region. Its people are deeply religious and accustomed to hard work. Like the earliest pioneers who braved droughts, dust storms, and rattlesnakes, Scurry County's current residents blend the common sense of an old Texas cowhand with their own unique brand of Southern hospitality.

If not born and raised in Snyder, one will constantly be asked, "Where are you from?" Many of the old timers still recall towns which can no longer be found on any map, some with particularly colorful names like "Hell Roarin' Hollar."

Scurry County is the kind of place where the tall tales of the American West merge with stories of modern oilfield roughnecks. Everywhere one looks are the last vestiges of genuine, small-town America. If one forgot to pay the bill at the local watering hole, the waitress will surely hand it back when walking in for coffee in the morning. Children play in the streets. Out in "the country" no one locks their doors. Looking for a farm truck? Someone "might could" lend one. The only thing more important than high school football is church on Sunday.

Of course, Scurry County has not always been so quiet. Snyder was once known as "Robber's Roost" and was the origin site of the last blood feud in Texas. There have been many colorful lawmen and more than a few "ornery cusses" over the years. In 1889, a man was caught cheating in a poker game, shot, and hung from a nearby tree.

More than outlaws and gunfighters, it was the buffalo hunters who defined this area. The Kiowa, Apache, and Comanche tribes hunted enormous herds of bison here. Quanah Parker is known to have wintered his tribe on Deep Creek. US Army "Indian Fighters" including Cpt. R.B. Marcy, Gen. Ranald Mackenzie, and a very young Robert E. Lee all left their footprints somewhere out on the plains, though the paths they walked have long been forgotten.

Arguably, Scurry County's most beloved resident was J. Wright Mooar. In his lifetime, Mooar was well acquainted with many men who eclipsed him in fame, including Buffalo Bill. Mooar shot a white buffalo on Deep Creek in 1876, an event which cemented his reputation as one of the greatest buffalo hunters of his era. True white buffalo are approximately one in 10 million, so rare that Pres. Theodore Roosevelt reportedly offered Mooar more than $5,000 for the hide. That is around $125,000 in today's money!

From the 1870s until 1949, Scurry County remained dependent on ranching and cotton farming, sustaining only a very small population of 4,000 permanent residents. Then, the discovery of more than four billion barrels of oil in the Canyon Reef formation caused Snyder's population to increase to more than 15,000 in less than a year! Dirt-poor cotton farmers became millionaires overnight. Among many other celebrities, Bob Hope and Don Ameche held claims in Scurry County.

After the first major oil boom ended, many residents departed for greener pastures. Determined not to let the bust get the best of them, those who stayed in Snyder joined forces for a citywide clean up and revitalization. They beat out contenders from all over the US and earned themselves a spotlight in *Look Magazine* along with the title of "Sparkle City" in 1968. The glitz and glitter of Sparkle City faded over time, as such things inevitably do—but Scurry County refused to bust again. It has marched on in the face of economic and environmental hardship, drawing in new industries while clinging to its farming and ranching roots. Today, the past and the future exist side by side, cattle grazing in the shadow of 300-foot-tall wind turbines, which produce green energy for cities hundreds of miles away.

One

BUFFALO DAYS

The history of Scurry County begins with the bison. In prehistoric times, this region was inhabited by millions of bison antiiqus, the predecessor of the American bison (bison bison). Though these animals are commonly called buffalo, they are more closely related to the extinct ancestors of modern cattle. Other prehistoric animals of West Texas included the Columbian mammoth, giant land tortoises, and the tiny ancestors of the modern horse. Paleontologists working in Scurry County have excavated an ancient riverbed filled with the remains of these animals. Archaeologists have found sites of human habitation dating back thousands of years. Stone tools and petroglyphs were discovered at Greene Springs and many ranchers have uncovered fossils or arrowheads on their property. Scurry County's first human residents were dependent on the buffalo for sustenance. In many Native American cultures the animal was attributed sacred status, and rare white buffalo were credited with possessing magical powers. The first Europeans were impressed by the enormous herds that roamed the plains. Conquistadors looking for cities of gold described seeing "seas of grass" filled with "immense herds of bison."

No-Co-Nie Comanches are pictured at Ta-Her-Ye-Qua-Hip, or horseback camp. Peta Nocona, Quanah Parker's father, was the chief of this band. (Photograph courtesy of W.S. Soule, March 22, 1873. Library of Congress.)

Of all of the Native American tribes who hunted bison in Scurry County, the Comanche were the most powerful and well organized. Comanche chief Quanah Parker was the leader of the Quahadi (Antelope) band, the last Comanche band to surrender to the US Army. Quanah's mother, Cynthia Ann Parker, was an Anglo American captured as a child and raised by the Comanche. Quanah Parker is known to have wintered his tribe in Scurry County. General Mackenzie and the US Army searched for Quanah Parker along Deep Creek but never captured him. Faced with starvation, Quanah surrendered in 1875 and led his band onto a reservation in Oklahoma. Widely respected by both Native American and Anglo leaders, Quanah was a leader in the Native American Church movement and was friends with Pres. Theodore Roosevelt.

The extermination of the buffalo was the single most important factor leading to the defeat of the Comanche and other powerful tribes of the Great Plains. Born in Vermont on August 10, 1851, J. Wright Mooar began his buffalo hunting career in Kansas. He sent some hides to his older brother John W. Mooar in New York, who sold them for $3.50 each. Over the next eight years, the brothers killed and marketed over 22,000 buffalo.

On the afternoon of October 7, 1876, J. Wright Mooar shot a rare albino buffalo near Deep Creek in Scurry County, an event that has become famous. He displayed the hide in his home, turning down lucrative offers from many prospective buyers—including Pres. Theodore Roosevelt. Mooar lived the rest of his life in Scurry County and died in 1940. The white buffalo hide still resides in Scurry County in the home of Judy Hays, his granddaughter. Pictured around 1900 are J. Wright Mooar (left) and John W. Mooar.

Gen. William Read Scurry was born in Gallatin, Tennessee, on February 10, 1821. He came to Texas in 1840. Scurry enlisted as a private during the Mexican War (1846–1847) and served in the Civil War on the side of the Confederacy, rising to the rank of brigadier general. Scurry was mortally wounded April 30, 1864, in the battle of Jenkins Ferry on the Sabine River. Scurry County was created in 1876 from Bexar County and organized on June 28, 1884, with the town of Snyder as the county seat. (Courtesy of *The Photographic History of the Civil War, Volume 10.* New York: The Review of Reviews Co., 1910.)

Following the Civil War, many veterans took advantage of cheap land in West Texas. Pictured at this January 1, 1905, "Old Soldier's Day" reunion are members of Bill Scurry Camp No. 1374 of the United Confederate Veterans. Pictured are D.P. Lane (man with flag), ? Garner (man without hat), and George "Kin" Elkins (the third man, back row). The two band men on the right are Ed Thompson and A.P. "Perm" Morris. Other men listed are A.B. Stiles, S.V. Sumruld, T.F. Rodman, J. Tinker, G. Johnson, J.M. Champion, W.R. Sharp, H.H. Merritt, M.A. Garden, T.D. McMillan, R.B. Robinson, J. Middleton, W.L. Stiles, Capt. A.B. Faver, R.G. Jones, R.A. Wilkerson, Rev. D.H. Burt, J.P. Gratham, W.R. Doak, J. Brown, Capt. A.J. Scarborough, R.J. Strayhorn, S. Sterrett, M.S. Teters, W.D. Brown, G. Garner, J.S. Jones, D. Trevey, W.M. Morton, D. Murphree, P.H. Morris, T. Lindley, T.C. Stinson, G.A. Glenn, W.D. Meador, R.J. Ware, F.M. German, D.B. Bynum, H.A. Goodwin, Capt. J.A. Clark, W.J. Fuller, J.K. Keller, C.E. Smith, G.J. Morgan, W.D. Huffman, Rev. L.D. Knight, J.M. Temple, W.A. Jones, and A.J. Goodwin.

Pictured are William Henry "Pete" and Nellie Snyder. In the early 1870s, buffalo hunters like J. Wright Mooar camped along Deep Creek and built dugouts on the creek banks. The settlement was originally called Hide Town. William Henry "Pete" Snyder took advantage of the remote location and started a trading post. Pete Snyder's store was the beginning of the county seat of Scurry County. On November 21, 1885, the post office was established and the town was officially named Snyder.

These two girls, Hattie Gatlin and Lucy Gillum Whitefield, are standing in front of Pete Snyder's dugout. The entrance was on Big Sulphur Creek. Lucy was beloved by the Snyders who called her "Baby." Her father, Z.P. Gillum, lived at Hell Roarin' Hollar near Dunn.

The Comanche in this photograph came into the young town of Snyder to have their photograph taken, probably around 1900. When local photographer H.V. Williams informed them of how long it would take for him to develop this photograph, they rode away without waiting for it. (Courtesy of the H.V. Williams family, Keith Pitner.)

The individuals in this tintype are believed to be members of the Beaver family of Fluvanna who arrived in Scurry County before 1899. A six-shooter was a necessity when Comanche attacks were still common. The violin was also a necessity. With miles between neighbors, a skilled musician could keep his or her family in high spirits despite the isolation of frontier life. There is a Scurry County story about how one desperate father, too proud to accept charity, sacrificed his one valuable possession, a violin, in order to buy food for his children. Whether this story is true or not—and what ultimately became of the poor musician's violin—is not known.

Roads of any kind were an unheard of luxury in early day in West Texas. Newcomers arrived by wagon in the days preceding the railroad. This is the road up Fluvanna Hill leading from Snyder to Post in the days before pavement.

Knapp Post office started in 1890

Small communities blossomed up on the plains all over Scurry County. The full dugout, which operated as the post office in the town of Knapp from 1890 until 1958, is pictured here.

Pyron had plans to expand to a size that would have rivaled Snyder. The town was founded in 1900 and moved four miles in 1910 to meet the Santa Fe Railroad. However, when the highway bypassed it, the town began to decline. The post office closed in 1958. Today, nothing remains of Pyron except for its historical marker. Texas author Jane Gilmore Rushing's book *Starting from Pyron* chronicles her experiences growing up in this town.

Named for Ira Green, who had a crossroads store near the townsite, Ira is located roughly eight miles from Snyder. The first homes and school were half-dugouts with windows set above ground level. On the opening of block 97 to settlers in 1899, Ira became an active farm and ranch community. This photograph was taken in 1911. The two-story building on the left was the grocery store, and upstairs was the Masonic lodge.

Dr. A.C. Leslie made house calls on horseback for most of his career. Though he looks more like a ranch hand than a physician in this photograph, he was a widely respected and competent doctor who provided a much-needed service in Scurry County.

Following the extermination of the buffalo, but before the days of barbed wire, cowboys on long cattle drives were a common sight in Scurry County. In 1880, a cow that might sell for $4 in West Texas was worth $25 in Kansas and $40 in New York. Driving the animals to the nearest railhead sometimes took months. Cowboys worked long hours for very little pay. Pictured are cowboys surrounding a chuckwagon on the Renderbrook-Spade Ranch. Sitting on the ground to the left of the wagon is W.L. Ellwood, owner of the ranch. Also pictured from left to right are E. "Ching" Enyart, two unidentified men, John Layne, "Erdie" Wulfgen, Perry Bracey (cook), unidentified, and D.N. Arnett (manager from 1891 to 1912) is on the far right with the wolfhound. The original photograph belonged to Otto F. Jones of Colorado City.

Deep Creek was appropriately named. In this photograph are members of the Lon Grantham family. Two of the ladies in the buggy are Maggie Barnes and Mrs. Grantham. Lon Grantham is holding the horse. The speed with which the water moved was sometimes very dangerous. Ranchers were convinced that the water supply was limitless, and newspapers advertised the excellent quality of the available grazing. Though water was certainly available in the early days, those who were not fortunate enough to own land on Deep Creek had to find some way of accessing it where it lay deep underground. Windmills provided a steady supply of water and were soon a part of every frontier town.

First Monday was trading day in Scurry County, an occasion for the whole community to get together. People brought everything they had to sell to the Snyder square. The public windmill seen in this photograph provided water for horses and mules. The brick structure to the left is the first courthouse and the county's second jail. The first jail was a 10-foot-by-8-foot shed called a calaboose.

18

Two

SNYDER

One of the first and proudest accomplishments of the new city was the coming of the railroad. This steam engine, bought by the Roscoe, Snyder & Pacific Railroad, arrived in Snyder on July 7, 1908. The man in the black suit and hat is J.W. Green, construction foreman. The arrival of the railroad was celebrated with barbecue, baseball games, and a carnival atmosphere. Established through efforts of Gen. F.W. James and H.O. Wooten, the Roscoe, Snyder & Pacific Railroad only covered 31 miles. For a time, however, it was the wealthiest railroad in the country per mile of track. It served as a connecting link with the Santa Fe and Texas & Pacific Railroads and played major role in the Scurry County oil boom of the 1920s and 1940s, transporting essential oil field equipment. All engines were converted from steam to diesel power by 1956. The Roscoe, Snyder & Pacific Railroad was originally intended to stretch from Roscoe (Nolan County) all the way to California. Builder H.O. Wooten made it as far as Fluvanna and then completely ran out of money. Nevertheless, the trains continued to run into the early 1970s, a testament to the big dreams of a little town.

The first courthouse and jail, built out of locally fired brick in 1886, was the most substantial building for miles around. Pictured from left to right are Jim Nunn, "Old Man" Grant, unidentified, Houston Patterson, "Grandpa" Byrd, Frank Wilks, Ira Kutch (sheriff), Walter Grantham, unidentified, William Bell, Az Woody, and Oz Smith.

The first sheriff of Scurry County, William "Uncle Billy" Nelson, resigned from his position after only six months in 1884, disgusted at how lawless the county was. He arrested only one man in his tenure as sheriff, but he arrested him twice. Upset by the circumstances of his arrest, the man got together with some of his friends, tied up the sheriff, and then tried to set the jail on fire. In his old age, "Uncle Billy" went blind and was led back and forth to his job as county auditor by his dog, Trixie. When he passed away, he requested that she be buried at his feet.

The first city marshal, O.P. "Pack" Wolf, was photographed on Twenty-fourth Street and Avenue S. The job of a city marshal was similar to a modern chief of police. He was responsible for keeping the peace in town, which was sometimes a very difficult task. With the establishment of local law enforcement, the reputation of "Robber's Roost" began to improve. By the time the railroad arrived in 1908, the town of Snyder could pass itself off as respectable. It became the big city of Scurry County and remains so to this day.

Snyder's next big accomplishment after the railroad was the construction of the 1911 courthouse. This photograph shows "Picnic Day" in front of the 1911 courthouse, a photograph from 1912 by E.H. Higgenbotham. The round spaces on the top of the dome were meant for clocks, but the fledgling city never could afford them.

First State Bank.

The First State Bank was erected from 1907 to 1908 on site where the trail of US Cavalry general Ranald MacKenzie ran parallel to Deep Creek. First State Bank & Trust Co. closed in 1931. It has since housed many businesses, including Hugh Boren Insurance Company and *The Scurry County Times* newspaper. The building maintains its original floors, ceilings, and exterior today.

Since trees were scarce in Scurry County, some early settlers hauled their own lumber for building all the way from east Texas. Snyder Lumber Company was one of the first businesses in the area to sell construction materials locally. Many families were not able to afford the cost of building a wooden house, so they continued to live in dugouts even into the 1920s. Tepee poles found at abandoned Native American campsites were sometimes collected and used for fence posts.

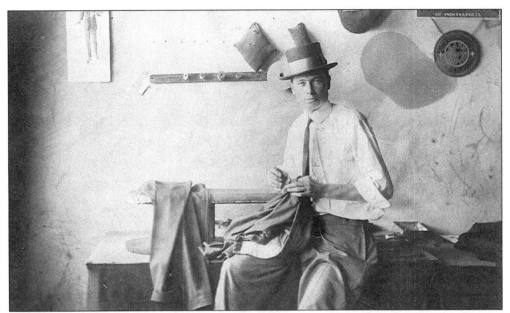

Bert Baugh's Tailor and Cleaning Shop was the first local steam press in Scurry County. Sewing machines had to be purchased and shipped from the east coast, which meant that many people made and repaired clothing by hand. Many Scurry County residents recall wearing clothing sewn from flour sacks when they were children. This photograph was most likely taken around 1910.

This photograph is of the Bert Smith Barber Shop. Pictured from left to right are Bert Smith, Bert Brown, and customer Boss Gail. The comforts of the big city followed the arrival of the railroads. Snyder was home to a confectionary, several theaters, stores that sold items from catalogs such as J.C. Penney, and barbershops. Frequenting a barbershop was sometimes considered evidence of bad morals and was notably forbidden for schoolteachers.

Every turn-of-the-century town was proud to assemble its own brass band. Members of Snyder's band included A.P. Morris, Monte Boren, Frank Boren, Jesse Thompson, L.D. Grantham, George Brown, and Andy Anderson. Local dentist Dr. Sed Harris played the tuba. This photograph shows a celebration at P.L. "Pie" Fuller's ranch in 1904.

There is barely a woman in sight in this image of Snyder Square around 1890. It was not unusual for frontier towns to be mainly populated by men. Men came to take advantage of work opportunities but did not marry or bring families in the early days. J. Wright Mooar, the buffalo hunter, did not himself marry until he was 50 years old. Following the coming of the railroads, the area was deemed civilized enough and more women began arriving. Early rancher Jim Nunn, who brought some of the first cattle to Scurry County in 1879, recalled that there was "no nothing" in Scurry County when he arrived. It was more than 30 miles to the nearest doctor, with no schools or churches. Over the course of a year, he claimed to have seen "only three women."

It was thought that women instinctively understood telephones better than men, so many early operators were women. Telephone companies usually served a small area and were locally owned and sometimes operated out of a person's house. One local operator recalled working at night without electricity. She used a candle stuck in a piece of corn bread to see which lines to connect. This telephone exchange was located in Hermleigh, and the photograph above dates from about 1920.

Though few women initially wanted to come to West Texas, small towns like Snyder actually afforded them opportunities for work. This 1912 photograph of the post office staff shows postmaster Katie Thrane (J.O. Nelson's wife) seated in the front row on the right. The other women are Mabel Clark (left) and Annie Moore (right). In the back, from left to right, are ? Freeman, J.O. Nelson, ? Farmer, and another employee.

Gladys Johnson and Ed Sims were only a few years away from a very nasty divorce in this 1910 photograph. An explosive encounter between Gladys and Ed on the Snyder Square on December 16, 1916, resulted in Gladys shooting her ex-husband with a pistol and her brother Sid finishing him off with a shotgun. The murder of Ed Sims, for which both Gladys and Sid were acquitted, marked the beginning of the Johnson-Sims feud, the last blood feud in Texas. In 1917, Gladys Johnson married Texas Ranger Frank Hamer, who is best known as the man who tracked down and killed the infamous gangsters Bonnie and Clyde.

District judge Cullen Higgins, the son of famous gunfighter Pink Higgins, was shot and killed because of his involvement in the Johnson-Sims feud. The March 22, 1918, *Snyder Signal* describes his murder: "Monday was opening day of district court in Clairemont and he was shot with a shotgun in the back from a window while he sat in the lobby of his hotel with Judge B. Thomas. Why was he murdered? We don't know . . . Perhaps he was in somebody's way?" Two thousand people attended his funeral.

Sports have always been a big part of life in Scurry County. Football is most definitely "king" today, but in the 1910s and 1920s baseball and basketball were much more popular. Ralph Hicks is pictured seated in front on the right. Also pictured are Bert Baugh, Rue Nation, Bud Dawson, Gus McClinton, John L. Webb, and three Woods brothers: Dick, Hendrix, and Cleve.

Girls played basketball as well, and Snyder High School had an undefeated girls' team in 1916. The photograph above is of Fluvanna High School in 1920. Did the girl with the ball make that free throw?

Fire was a constant danger in the days before electricity. This is the aftermath of the fire on April 12, 1908, which took place between First State Bank and Keith's Confectionary. Three years later, a fire at Snyder Mercantile Company would burn this side of the square again.

In 1916, Snyder firemen acquired their first truck, complete with buckets, ladders, and a chemical pressure tank—a big step forward from horse-drawn equipment. Fire chief H.G. Towle is at the steering wheel.

W.T. Baze and his assistant are working in his blacksmith shop. The Baze family was among early arrivals to Scurry County and the blacksmith shop provided every service from horseshoeing to the production of essential frontier tools.

Another member of the Baze family, J.I. Baze, was photographed with a 100-horsepower motor at Snyder Ice, Light, and Power, which provided the first electricity in the area.

J. Nelson Dunn's Confectionary operated from 1928 to 1959. A confectionary would usually offer candies, chips, pretzels, soda, and ice cream. It might also sell things like cigarettes, magazines, and comic books.

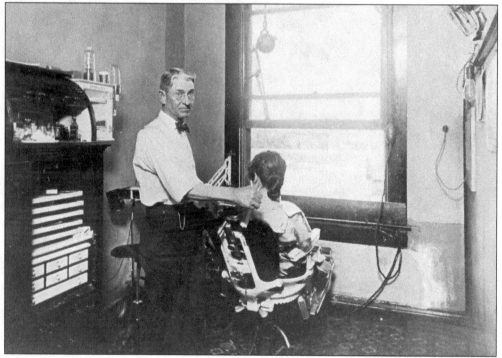

Dr. Sed Harris practiced dentistry in Snyder from 1898 to 1941. One might imagine that he did a very good business with a practice located so close to Dunn's Confectionary.

Horses and buggies were slowly replaced by cars. This livery stable was formerly located on Avenue Q and Twenty-fourth Street. It housed horses and mules to be rented out and also offered a Jersey bull and a Missouri jack for breeding. Bicycles became increasingly popular in the early part of the century, and two can be seen in the background of this photograph.

In her 1926 high school scrapbook, lifelong Snyder resident Mary Lynn Nation Scott listed automobiles as one of the top things that "both boys and girls like." While the older generation was apprehensive about cars when they began arriving in the 1910s, by the time this photograph was taken, Snyder had become a miniature motor city. Pictured from left to right are Doris Buchanan, Rowena Grantham, Marge Dell Prim, Audrey Wasson, R.W. (Dick) Webb, Nelson Dunn (owner of the local candy shop), and toddler Bobby Baugh.

This is an artist's depiction of one of the first intercity buses in the United States. Snyder resident W.B. Chenoweth, who also registered one of the first cars in Scurry County, designed a six-cylinder engine and a chain drive, which would propel the vehicle at nearly 25 miles per hour. He tried to sell his design but was rudely informed that he "must have been kicked in the head by a mule" if he thought that he would be allowed to operate a "self-propelled vehicle on a public road." On October 29, 1907, Chenoweth began bus service from Colorado City to Snyder. Preachers were so worried about the dangers of the bus that they warned their congregations not to ride on it. When Chenoweth offered free passage, five daring souls made the trip to Colorado City. Citizens soon passed a resolution forbidding the bus to be driven in Snyder, and Chenoweth moved his business to Big Spring.

The arrival of the airplane heralded a whole new era. Fine weather in West Texas for flying caused the region to produce many pilots between 1929 and 1945. Avenger Field in nearby Sweetwater was the training center for WASP (Women's Air Service Pilots) during World War II. Pictured from left to right are W.W. Hamilton, Bill Hamilton, H.G. Towle, Joe Caton, R.D. English, Bill Doake, J.W. ?, Walt Scott, D.P. Yoder, Ernest Taylor, C. Wedgeworth, Andy Anderson, J.C. Stinson, Herman Darby, O.P. Thrane, Henry Rosenburg, ? Garner, Ed Thompson, and Pat Bullock.

Three

CHURCHES

Founded in May 1883, one year before Scurry County was organized, First Baptist was originally named Bledsoe Baptist Church in the honor of John S. Bledsoe, one of the founders. The first pastor, Rev. J.G. Garrard, served from 1883 to 1890. At that time, worship was held in the school building on alternate Sundays. A lot in the original Snyder townsite was purchased for a church in 1892 and has remained the site of four consecutive church buildings. The first was a one-story 40-foot-by-60-foot frame building with a bell tower. In 1922, a brick building was constructed on the site. In its years of existence, First Baptist has begun many missions which have become organized churches in their own right. The Avenue D. Baptist and Greenhill Baptist Churches are two of these. Colonial Hill Baptist Church was organized by several members from First Baptist. Early-day pastors traveled by buggy to preach in Longhorn Valley, Sulphur Creek, and Pleasant Ridge. This photograph shows First Baptist Church as it appears today. A major addition was added to the First Baptist building site in 1977. The present church seats more than 1,000 people. First Baptist celebrated its 125th anniversary in 2008 and remains a powerful driving force in Scurry County.

This photograph shows a First Baptist Church baptism in 1908. Brother Ingram, the pastor, and Brother Johnson, the evangelist, are in the foreground. One of the women in the water is Gertrude Fondy Murphree.

Deep Creek was the site of many baptisms. This 1913 photograph shows a summer baptism near the Twenty-fifth Street Bridge.

Both social and church-related women's groups have existed since around 1900. The name Sunday school class may be misleading, for these groups were typically composed of adult women who would take part in community outreach and raise money for various causes. They did have some religious instruction, usually from a deacon in the church which is why there is often one man seated in the middle of the group. This photograph shows the Phylathee Sunday school class and teacher Fred Grayum between 1912 and 1917.

This c. 1923 photograph is of the Althean Sunday school class at First Baptist Church. This class commonly met at the Watkins family home, which was originally the Howell home at Avenue U and Twenty-seventh Street. Pictured from left to right are Alma Watkins, Goldie West, ? Stoker (Guy's mother), ? Williamson, ? Blackard, ? Evans, ? Cobb, ? Cobb (child), ? Taylor, ? Taggart, ? Chinn (Sunday school teacher whose husband was the city marshal), Mrs. Oscar Spear, ? Autry (Leon's mother), Mrs. Ada Martin, ? Blackard or ? Williams, ? Ross, Micah Martin, ? Keith, ? Hamilton, Mrs. S.J. Brice, Mrs. Morrow (Jim Stinson's sister), Lila Guinn (not from Hermleigh), Bea Faulkner, ? Cook, ? Northcutt, Lottie Shuler, unidentified, Mrs. W.W. Patterson, and five unidentified women.

The original 1902 sanctuary was located on the same site as the present church. This photograph was taken from the north side of Twenty-seventh Street by Mrs. F.J. Grayum, whose young son Billy is watering her front yard.

First Methodist Church was organized in July 1883 by Rev. R.F. Dunn at the request of B.L. Patterson during a revival on Ennis Creek. The first one-room church was built on land donated by T.N. Nunn in 1889. It was used until 1910, when the congregation grew too large. Services were then held in the courthouse. In 1914, during the ministry of Rev. J.W. Hunt, a red brick church with a dome replaced the one-room building. The present sanctuary was built in 1961, and the building in the image above was demolished.

First Christian Church was organized in 1898 with eight charter member families. The first building was erected on Deep Creek on land donated by A.C. Wilmeth. Some members had to wade the creek in order to get to church after it rained. The building was originally octagonal in shape and was known as "Little Round Church." In 1950, the congregation doubled after the oil discovery. The present church was erected in 1953, and the historic church was demolished.

First Presbyterian Church was organized on June 13, 1892, as the First Cumberland Presbyterian Church, by Rev. W.W. Werner. It used a basement at Avenue R and Twenty-eighth Street for worship until this sanctuary was completed in 1929. Leaded stained-glass memorial windows honor a small, dedicated congregation who built this church. A bell forged in 1902 was still used regularly during the 1960s.

A March 16, 1934, gathering was photographed at the congregation of The Church of God and Christ. In the front row, third from right, is Vernest Tippens. In the back row, the first on the left with suit jacket, hat, and tie is Rev. H. Norris. African American churches were established when the Depression attracted newcomers working in the cotton industry.

Mount Olive parishioners were active in the Masons and Eastern Star. These women are gathered for an Eastern Star Ceremony in 1952. Pictured from left to right are Loretta ?, Rebecca James, Elosie Newsome, Bessie Newsome, ? Johnson, Lilly Archer, Annie Dee Hunter, Magnolia Choyce, Johnny Faye Clay, Lena Nelson, and Mary Baker. Mount Olive was established in April 1926, and Reverend Culpepper was its first pastor.

These children were photographed after receiving their first communion at St. Xavier Catholic Church, which later became St. John's.

St. John's Catholic Church in Hermleigh was the first parish to be founded in the diocese of Lubbock. The brick building in this photograph replaced the original wooden building in 1939 and still stands today. Identified in the photograph are the following parishioners and their families: Frank Watzl, Rosie Williams, Frank Zalman, John Zalman II, Bill Zimmerman, John Bartels, Anton Brom, Jacob Brom, Charlie Cizek, Anton Freytag, Duke Grossman, Rosemarie Goebel, Walter Goebel, Joe Hundsmercher, Herman Hundsmercher, Charlie Hilcher, Otto Hoepfl, Albert Kuss Sr., Albert Kuss Jr., Joe Kuss, Frank Kuss, Mathis Kuss, A.J. Kuss, Edwin Kuss, Alvin Kuss, E. Kuss, Frank Kubala, Willie Kubena, Jim Kubena, Rudy Kubena, Fred Kashper, Winford Light, Frank Mackard, Ted Minels, Joe Nachlinger, John Neitzler, John Pavlicek, Dalmon Pieper, Edd Parilas, Gary Pieper, Joe Roemisch, John Roemisch, Johnnie Roemisch, Jimie Frank Roemisch, Albert Joe Roemisch, Charlie Richter, Edmon Richter, Frank Senhersch, Herman Schulze, Robert Schulze, H.J. Schulze, Willie Schulze, Emil Schulze, Frank Schulze, Ben Seinenberger, Henry Wimmer, Alfonse Wimmer, Bill Wimmer, Emil Wimmer, Bennie Mray, Russel Mray, George Mray, Frank Wenetschlager, Paul Wenetschlager, and Herman Wenetschlager.

This photograph shows the First Baptist Church in Fluvanna around 1958. Because of the scarcity of wood in Scurry County, building a frame church was a major undertaking. Before a sanctuary could be constructed, church members met in homes, business, at the courthouse, the school, and even outdoors. Some of the earliest churches were very small and soon outgrown by their congregations. Very few of these churches still stand today. Most were replaced in the 1950s or after, when the oil boom made more space a necessity.

In 1950, Union Baptist Church had its own oil company, a sign of the changing times.

Four

FARMS AND RANCHES

Before the 1949 discovery of the Canyon Reef oilfield put Scurry County on the map, the region's most important industries were cotton and cattle. There is some contention over which local rancher can truly claim to have brought the first cattle to Scurry County, but most agree that James Nunn did so in 1879. The Webb family brought cattle around the same time. Without competition from the vast herds of buffalo which had once roamed West Texas, cattle thrived. Cotton, long a staple of the Southern economy, had some trouble getting started in Scurry County. Though the soil provided adequate conditions, storms damaged cotton crops before they could be harvested. Enterprising Scurry Countian Clemens Von Roeder solved this problem by breeding a better strain of cotton, rugged enough to withstand West Texas wind. Today, it is known as "Western Stormproof" and is widely grown throughout Texas and many other places as well.

Spring branding is pictured on the Renderbrook-Spade Ranch. By 1887, the Renderbrook Ranch encompassed 300,000 acres (1,200 km2) in four counties, primarily Mitchell County. Some of the cowboys in this photograph probably rode the range 25 miles north in Scurry County in the days before barbed wire. Pictured are Sam Moreland, Sid Rowe, U.D. "Erdie" Wulfgen or Wulfjen, E. (Ching) Enyart (holding head of calf), John W. Cathey, George Latty, and an unidentified cowboy.

A herd of cattle probably belonging to Roger Mize stands guard around the windmill, which provided them with water.

The first cows in Texas were longhorns. In this photograph, three cowboys rope a longhorn in the stock pens near Fuller Cotton Mill around 1915. Other men watch on the sidelines and sit on the fence. Longhorns are still considered by many to be the iconic Texas steer. They were hardy and could survive on less grazing and water. When it no longer was necessary to take cattle on long drives to the railroad, it became preferable to raise animals which produced more meat. Driving the highways of West Texas today, it is a rare sight to see a genuine longhorn.

Some registered shorthorn cows were bought from Ervie and shipped to Fort Worth around 1910. These were the earliest breed of cattle raised by Wade and Harrie Winston.

Harrie Winston surveys his Hereford cattle. Snyder's airport is named Winston Field. The Winston family came to Scurry County in 1907 so that Harrie and Wade could attend a better school. At the end of that year, the brothers began trading cattle. This was the beginning of a partnership that would last until Wade's death in 1958. The Winston family left the cattle business after Harrie's death in 1974 and generously donated to many local institutions, including Colonial Hill Baptist Church, Winston Field, and the Scurry County Museum.

A. Parsons and Dwight Monroe sit atop an enormous load of hay around 1908.

The Johnson boys are pictured sitting on horses at W.R. "Bill" Johnson Ranch. The boys are, from left to right, Emmett, Sid, unidentified, Joe, and unidentified. Emmet, Sid, and Joe are the brothers of Gladys Johnson, who famously ignited the Johnson-Sims feud by shooting her husband Ed Sims on the Snyder Square in 1916. This photograph was probably taken between 1905 and 1910.

These unidentified cowboys are pictured branding calves. The photograph was collected by the Scurry County Genealogical Society.

Hugh Taylor and a bull are seen here. The Taylor family is one of the oldest families in Scurry County. In addition to ranching, they have owned and operated a number of businesses in Snyder including a grocery store, a sports equipment store, and a computer repair shop.

Bob Watlington proudly displays Studebaker, his grand champion steer. Studebaker certainly drew a lot of attention at the State Fair of Texas in 1949. The tie that Watlington is wearing is embroidered with his steer's portrait.

Barrel racer Jamie
Bean gallops down
the home stretch.

Dave Appleton came
from Australia to ride
for Western Texas
College Rodeo in 1981.
This photograph was
published on the cover of
College Rodeo Magazine
in December 1982.

Pictured around 1900 is the P.L. "Pie" Fuller Ranch, located north of Snyder. At one time, P.L. and his brother owned over 1,000 sections of land.

This c. 1980 photograph shows the old barn on the P.L. "Pie" Fuller's Ranch.

Farm and ranch life was not limited to raising cotton and cattle. In this photograph, Ben Hamilton is seen butchering hogs. The young girl is his daughter, Gertrude (Trudy) Hamilton Summerall. Ben Hamilton's wife, Pearl DeShazo Hamilton, came from a family who were early-day residents of the Camp Springs and Hermleigh area.

Nothing says West Texas like some genuine barbecue. Pictured are H.J. Brice and several men standing around a barbecue pit.

An unidentified family poses in front of their ranch house in Scurry County.

This Snyder store, originally called Fullilove & Monroe and later J. Monroe Hardware, sold buggies, windmills, and piping. In front of the store in this c. 1912 photograph, several horse-drawn planters are displayed. Next-door was Wenninger & Sons Grocery.

Originally located about five miles northeast of Snyder, the Harrell house was moved to the National Ranching Heritage Center in Lubbock in 1972. The house began as one room built in 1883 by R.T. Mellard from stones picked up on Hackberry Creek. A box and strip wing was added between 1901 and 1912 by the Lon Smith family. In its heyday, the house was pretty fancy. The house was also home to the O.W. Reynolds family. It was in the possession of the Harrells beginning in 1934.

As a child, Fay Harrell rode with her father and twin brother, helping with ranch affairs while Myrtle Harrell helped her mother around the house. Both sisters became teachers, although after only two years of teaching, Fay declared that she would "rather teach cows 365 days a year." When their father could no longer maintain his ranch, the sisters ran it together. In this photograph, Fay and Myrtle Harrell stand in the kitchen of their house after it was moved to the National Ranching Heritage Center.

A coal-burning threshing machine works its way through a crop of maize around 1910 or 1912.

Cotton wagons lined up at the Joyce Gin in Snyder. Around 1931, gins were powered by steam. Oil and coal used for fuel. Note the smokestack on the far left.

Pictured in the winter of 1926 are Mert Patterson, Riley Austin, Carl Keller, Roy Jones, Bill Crowder, Red Hassell, Charley Morrow (standing on tractor), ? Day, and Simon Best (on tractor).

Clemens Von Roeder moved to Scurry County in 1907. By 1923, he was producing a long staple, big boll cotton, and had introduced strains to resist hail, windstorms, and rust. He was joined by his brother Nolan in 1934 and by Bentley Baize, an agricultural executive, in 1940. Nolan's son Max joined the family business in 1957 and still resides in Scurry County today. Von Roeder marketed seeds are Texas Mammoth and Western Prolific for handpicking and Western Stormproof for modern mechanical harvesting. Pictured are Bentley Baize and Nolan Von Roeder.

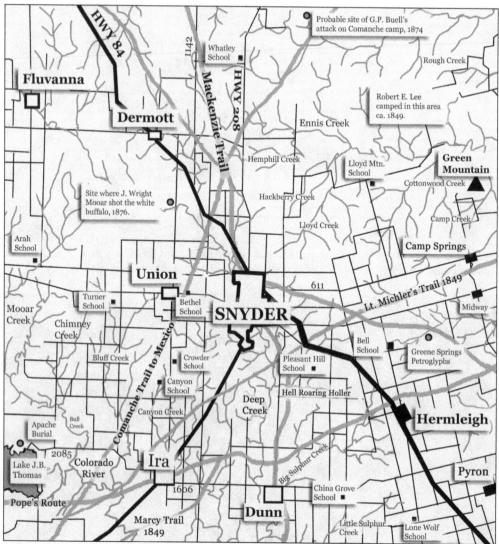

This map of Scurry County shows the locations of many of the small farming and ranching communities, many of which no longer have any residents. Apart from Snyder (population 10,653), only Fluvanna (population 180), Hermleigh (population 393), Dunn (population 75), and Ira (population 250) still have post offices. Since the 1800s, a post office was often the first business to open in a town and the last one to close before the area was abandoned.

Alvin Hill is pictured ginning cotton in 1985. The kind of gin he is standing in front of came into use in the 1890s, and though the source of power used to drive the gin changed from steam to electricity in the 1940s and 1950s, the basic mechanism remained the same.

Bales of cotton are ready to be transported. The Roscoe, Snyder & Pacific Railroad, which ran through Scurry County, provided a vital link between the West Coast and the Santa Fe Railroad in Sweetwater. Goods could travel all the way from Dallas to California, switching trains in Snyder. This was very important to the cotton industry.

Many ranchers in Scurry County also raised goats or sheep. These women are bottle-feeding the lambs.

The children playing with these puppies are W.J. Murphree Jr., Dorothy Murphree Rosson, and Elsie Murphree Tippen, probably around 1925. Their parents, Will Murphree and Gertrude Fondy, married in 1915 and farmed in Scurry County.

The Beaver family is pictured near Fluvanna where they farmed. Three generations were raised on the same section of land. Three helpers are also pictured with grandfather N. Beaver, Kate (an eccentric relative), Lena, Travis, Della (Lewis's wife), Lila Lee, Stella, and Odyne.

Seen here is Uncle Lois Caton's house around 1900, located around eight miles north of Snyder on the Clairemont Road. Nancy Caton was a Dodson and the aunt of Ella Eubanks. Many of the earliest families to settle in Scurry County came because their relatives were already in the area.

Monroe Tomhakara, grandson of Quanah Parker, Robert Taylor (sculptor), and Judy Hays, granddaughter of J. Wright Mooar, at the unveiling of the white buffalo statue on the Snyder square in 1994.

Judy Hays is seen here as a child with her grandfather J. Wright Mooar. Mooar did not marry until he was 50 years old and never had any children with his wife, but they adopted Judy's father, Thomas McDonald. Famous in her own right for her Circle H brand quarter horses, which include Dr. Te, Gann's Three Chick, 15 grand champions, and 12 AQHA champions, Judy Hays inherited the land on which J. Wright Mooar built his ranch. It is still in the possession of the Hays family, and the hide of the famous white buffalo is in Judy's home.

Five

READING, WRITING, ARITHMETIC, AND FOOTBALL

Most of the small communities in Scurry County had their own one room schoolhouses where children attended first through eighth grade. Besides the basics of reading, writing, and arithmetic, school sports have long played an important role in community life. Football arrived fairly early in Scurry County, beginning in 1923. It has been enormously popular ever since, and Snyder High School has produced a number of exceptional players who have gone on to college and professional careers. This is the school in Wheat (Hermleigh) around 1905. Pictured from left to right are (first row) Oliver Corley, Champ Freeman, Robert Freeman, Martin Freeman, George Peterson, Edgar Echols, Bill Rea, two unidentified students, and Hubert Rea; (second row) Pinnix Echols, Boblee Coke, Clyde Rea, Moze Corley, Homer Adams, Claude Freeman, John Sturdivant, Will Echols, Birtie Appleton, Roy Coston, Cleave Mixon, and Luther McJemsey; (third row) Gertrude Herm, McJemsey, Era Coker, Edna Gannaway, unidentified, Mrs. Hicks Copeland, Hicks Copeland (teacher), Occo Echols, Lelia Coket, Ethel Gannaway, Laura Shipman, Eunice Appleton, Eva Paul, and Flossie Cliff; (fourth row) Hattie Herm, unidentified, Doll Peterson, Ready Rea, May Appleton, Etheal Paul, Nannie Appleton, Edith Cliff, unidentified, Howard Clemons, Aubry Webb, Tom Coker, unidentified, and Ray Cliff; (fifth row) Ethel Shipman, May Freeman, Edith Hopper, May McJemsey, unidentified, Birdie Peterson, Eunice Rea, Bessie Webb, Vida Wasson (teacher), Pearl Cliff, Eva Appleton, Lela Mixon, Pearl Derby, and Ruth Shipman.

Like many other Scurry County towns, there is very little left of Camp Springs today. Originally visited by Native Americans and later by the US Army, Camp Springs was a thriving community with its own schoolhouse by 1903. In this photograph, teacher Emma Snuffer is seated on the bottom right. The two children nearest to her are Maggie and Callin Boone.

Another early school was Cottonwood, where Jim Middleton taught in 1900. Though many elementary teachers were women, it was thought that men made better teachers for older students because they could discipline them more effectively. Punishments in 1900 might include smacking the pupil's knuckles with a ruler, spanking them with a cane or paddle, making them stand in the corner, or sending them outside to pound the chalk from erasers.

This picture shows J.W. (Florence) Leftwich teaching at the Bell School southeast of Snyder in 1904. It was the first school that she taught at over the course of her very long career. The classroom was for grades one through eight, and the total enrollment was 27.

This photograph shows the first-grade class at Hermleigh, where J.W. Leftwich also taught.

This is an early photograph of Egypt School, located south of Ira. Carrie Bowers was the teacher at the time.

Zada Maxwell is pictured with her class at West Ward School. The names listed on the back of this photograph are Nancy C., Lena M., Dora, Merle, Ruby, Carrie, Elsie, Mavis, Eleanor, Rosalie, Ruby, Ethel L., Janice, Mermie, Mable D., Lillian W., Clare Bell, Louise T., Mamie C., Lola, Claud W., Edd Burditt, Louis Blackard, Hurbert Baze, Harrey Daniels, Arthur, G.B. Clark, Harvey White, Tracy Smith, Ralph Johnson, Berry, unidentified, Bell Borns, and Canon Burditt.

Fifth- and sixth-grade Ira School students were photographed on March 13, 1914. Students are, from left to right, Neal Hardee (1), Sidney Young (2), Newell Beard (3), Butler Barnett (4), Ethel Robison (5), Rosa Sorrells (6), Eula Camp (7), Clara Taylor (8), Nellie Wright (9), Susie Hardee (10), Essie Taylor (11), Wayne Holley (12), Calude Holley (13), Bird Carlile (14), Buster Rhoades (15), Robbie Hewett (16), Weldon Stinson (17), Linnie Taylor (18), Gertie Chambers (19), Exa Sorrells (20), Lorena Wright (22), Bernice Lamberth (22), Alpia Knox (23), and Maybel Taylor (24).

The Ira School House around early 1900 and a group of men who built it are seen here.

High School.

The first brick school in Scurry County, Snyder High School, was built between 1904 and 1905. The school was located on Twenty-sixth Street and Avenue M. This building burned in 1922, was rebuilt in the mid-1920s, and burned again in 1938. It was rebuilt and used in different capacities. Eventually, it became Travis Junior High School. It was torn down in 1975, and the Scurry County Jail and sheriff's office were built on the site.

The Travis Gymnasium, constructed by the Works Progress Administration from local river rock, is still located on the site of the original Snyder High School.

West Ward School was located near the water tank on Thirty-second Street. Like North Ward School, it was built around 1908 to 1910, but the railroad did not bring as many people to Scurry County as residents hoped it would. Both West Ward and North Ward were abandoned and torn down by 1921.

This 1913 class photograph of West Ward School's fifth-grade class includes Grace Moore, Porter King (teacher), Lois Sears Sentell, M. Morrow, Inez Baze Brown, Elaine Davis Mellard, Loree Stokes Dodson, Dimple Gross Stokes, Francis Harris, Merle Johnston Williams, Marietta Longbotham, Floy Davis Head, and Clay Eppley.

This is a 1928 image of the old Dermott School, which is now located at the Heritage Village in Snyder. The students are, from left to right, (first row) W.C. Sanders, T.L. Wilson, Almer Patrick, A.J. Jordan, Ned Whatley, and Raymond Frisbie; (second row) W.F. ?, Patrick ?, Oliver Frisbie, W. Scrivner, Snookie Elkins, Marshall Johnson, La Verne Edmonson, Aline Gordon, Melvin Click, A. Freeman, Chas Woellert, and Vivian Davidson; (third row) W.T. Steele, Dorothy Way, Louie Johnson, Velma Lee Edmonson, Katherine Scrivener, Gladys C., Dorothy Mae Gordon, Evelyn S., Larlerie Greenfield, Arlene Freeman, ? Woellert, and Dayton McCarty; (fourth row) Corene Gordon, two unidentified students, L. Gordon, Edna ?, D. Way, Mary Woellert, A.D. Johnson, and Inez S.

School superintendent Nealy Squires is pictured in her office around 1925. She formerly taught at Camp Springs School beginning around 1915.

This group photograph shows the faculty of Central School Building in 1912. From left to right are (first row) Ethel Birch, Eula Davis, John Leftwich, ? Gable, and Ina Davis; (second row) unidentified, Gladys McCormick, Mary Heath, Florence Leftwich, Bessie Buchanan, Dasey Brady, Maude Williams, and Ola Bibbee.

Students in Florence Middleton Leftwich's class are pictured in 1910.

The undefeated Snyder High School girls' 1916 basketball team, pictured here with Coach Gavelt, included Lois Johnston (left), Bessie Garner, Maggie Wilson, and Leona Strayhorn.

The first effort at organized high school football in Snyder was in 1923 when Bill Falls coached the team. The players included Noel Banks, Iton Nicholas, John Carroll, A.D. Dodson, Wade Greene, Bernon Etheredge, A. Smith, Judd McGaha, Jesse Jones, Harvey Carroll, Sam Etheredge, ? Falls, N. Curry, Hollis Lloyd, Alph P., Watson Adans, and Ward Golden. The team operated from the Notre Dame box formation.

Ned Underwood and Keith Pitner were
football players for Snyder High who played
on the team between 1951 and 1953.

Samuel Adrian "Slingin' Sammy" Baugh played
professional football for the Washington Redskins
from 1937 to 1952. He won two NFL Championships
(1937 and 1942) and held every passing record.
The position of quarterback hardly existed when
Baugh began playing, and he set the standard.
He was inducted into the Pro Football Hall of
Fame in 1963 as one of the first 17 members.
After retiring from coaching, Baugh returned to
West Texas, where he spent the rest of his life. He
was a strong supporter of Western Texas College,
and the golf course is named in his honor.

Grant Teaff served as head coach at Baylor University from 1972 to 1992, compiling a career record of 170-151-8. He was inducted into the College Football Hall of Fame in 2001. Teaff played high school football at Snyder High School. The Baylor Bears football team had been 7-43-1 in the seasons preceding Teaff's arrival, but the 1974 Baylor Bears football team is referred to as the "Miracle on the Brazos." The team captured the Southwest Conference title that year. Teaff remained Baylor's coach until 1992 and compiled a winning record that included many bowl games and another Southwest Conference title in 1980. (Courtesy of Baylor Athletics.)

During the 1950s, Snyder High School had a very accomplished band program that won many awards. Pictured here are members of the 1955–1956 Snyder High School Stage Band and Class AAA champions.

Snyder High School Band won the Region II Sweepstakes in 1956 and 1957. Such a competition challenges some of the very best high school programs in the state to perform their best. The winning band, Snyder High School, had the honor of appearing at the Cotton Bowl.

Jerry Worsham began teaching drama at Snyder High School in 1966. He led his students to a record 13 state championships in one-act play competition, earning a distinction as the most successful theater director in UIL history. In fact, Worsham's record is unmatched by any coach or director of any sport or activity in Texas interscholastic history. Many of his students went on to have successful acting careers, including Barry Tubb, who is most famous for his role as Wolfman in the movie *Top Gun*. Worsham is pictured here with two of his students, Bryan Lewallen and Nell Sears, who achieved top billing at the University Interscholastic League Competition for their production of *Macbeth* in 1979.

The first school buses in Snyder began in the 1920s. Their arrival coincided with the closing of many of the small community schools such as Cottonwood, Bison, and Camp Springs. By 1940, a much more comprehensive bussing program was bringing children from all over Scurry County to attend school in Snyder. Some towns such as Hermleigh still have their own schools, but there were many more schools in Scurry County around 1920 than there are today.

Before public schools integrated in 1965, local African Americans attended the Lincoln School, located just north of Thirty-seventh Street. Those who attended the Lincoln School recall it fondly, explaining that the teachers encouraged them to excel and succeed. Some students encountered silent prejudice when the schools were first integrated. One Lincoln School alumna expressed that in her first days at Snyder High School, she realized that none of her teachers expected her to do well. Determined to prove them wrong, she graduated at the top of her class. Before the establishment of the Lincoln School, black students had to be bussed out of Scurry County if they desired to attend school past the eighth grade.

Six

FIGHTING TEXAS

The 36th Infantry Division was organized at Camp Bowie, Texas, in July 1917, and was formed from units of the Texas and Oklahoma National Guard. Some units saw combat in World War I, and many served in the occupation forces. By the time they were released from active duty in 1919, the division had adopted a shoulder patch consisting of a blue arrowhead with a green "T" superimposed over it. The arrowhead stood for Oklahoma, and the "T" stood for Texas. After the war, the 36th Infantry was reorganized and became an "all Texas" division known as the "T" patch. On November 25, 1940, the Division was mobilized for World War II. It landed in North Africa, and then in Italy at Paestum in 1943. The 36th Infantry was the first American combat division to land on the continent of Europe. The Division fought in the Italian Campaign as part of the 5th United States Army. Driving up through Southern France, the 36th Infantry was attacking and breaking the Siegfried Line when the war in Europe ended. The 36th Infantry had spent 400 days in combat, accepted the surrender of Field Marshal Hermann Goering, won seven campaign streamers, taken part in two assault landings, and 14 of its members had won the Medal of Honor. It also had the ninth highest casualty rate of any Army division in World War II. Many men from Scurry County served in Company G, 36th Infantry Division. Reunions were hosted at the Scurry County Museum for these men until too few veterans remained to continue organizing them. These soldiers are pictured in formation on the Snyder Square in 1944.

The man on the left in this photograph is Elmer Taylor, a World War I Scurry County pilot. During World War I, pilots were sometimes called "the knights of the air," because flying was seen as glamorous in comparison to the trenches. Pilots engaged in spectacular aerial dogfights, flying close enough to one another to fire pistols or throw objects because their planes were not outfitted with weapons.

This photograph of John F. Hodnett, Company F., 7th Division, 34th Infantry, was taken in Mt. Vernon, Texas, in 1918. The Hodnett family lived near Hermleigh.

In this c. 1918 photograph are Dr. W.R. Johnson (seated) and Dr. Hatfield.

These American soldiers, pictured in 1918 with a captured German gun, are believed to be members of the 37th Division.

This was one of the many scrap drives that took place in Snyder during World War II. The courthouse lawn was often piled high with scrap.

Wartime weddings were very common. Here, Ruby Lee is marrying B.L. McKinley before he ships off with the US Navy.

Mary Lynn Scott and a Mrs. D. Mitchell
of the Altrurian Daughters women's
club are pictured working a Women's
Auxiliary Army Corps (WAAC)
recruiting information booth.

Edith McKanna sits on the wing of an
airplane. McKanna was a member of
the 99 Club along with Amelia Earhart.
The club's membership consisted of the
first 99 women to receive their pilots'
licenses in the United States. Avenger
Field in nearby Sweetwater served as a
training ground for Women's Air Service
(WASP) pilots. Excellent flying weather
in West Texas drew courageous women
from all around the country. The chief
requirement was that they needed to
have a pilot's license already. They were
then trained to fly military aircraft so
that they could assist with transferring
planes wherever they were needed, pulling
targets for combat training and fulfilling
other necessary roles on the homefront.

John Portis was born and raised in Scurry County. Devoted to preserving the history of the area, he wrote extensively about the things he remembered from his childhood, such as the local OK Wagon yard. In this photograph taken during World War II, he is overseas in Algiers. While he is a long way from West Texas in this photograph, the hot, dry, dusty weather of North African desert does not seem to bother him at all.

Henry "Hank" Clark holds up a shadowbox containing his souvenirs from World War II. In 2005, interviewed by the *Snyder Daily News* 60 years after the end of the war, Henry spoke of witnessing one of his friends killed in a tank explosion and helping to gather the bodies of the dead at the Nordhausen concentration camp.

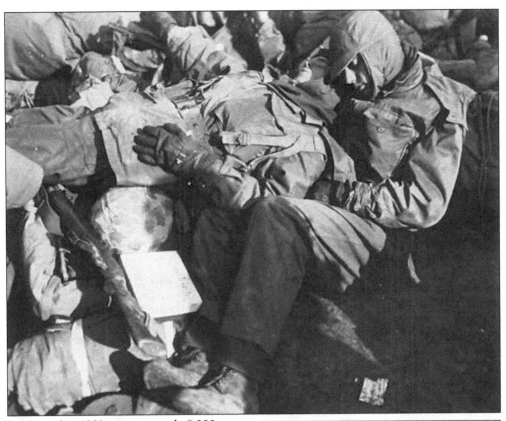

In November 1950, approximately 8,000 soldiers, most of them US Marines, struggled to survive the coldest winter in 100 years in North Korea. Surrounded by 120,000 Chinese soldiers, their only lifeline was a 15-inch wide, steep mountain road they called the MSR (Main Supply Route) that led to the port city of Hungnam. Scurry County veteran V.L. Buchanan recalls one soldier "grinning like a madman" when it was discovered that his frostbite was so severe that his toes would need to be amputated. "He knew that was his ticket home," Buchanan explained. He remembers the temperature as being "30 degrees below zero and even colder." (Courtesy of Wayne Merritt, Scurry County veteran.)

V.L. "Buck" Buchanan (right), also a Scurry County veteran of the Korean War, commanded a tank during the war. The man pictured with him was his driver.

William Paul Rollins was killed in action during the Vietnam War. He was awarded many medals, including the Distinguished Flying Cross.

The soldier second from right, not looking at the camera, is Lee Burke. After serving in the Vietnam War, Burke began working at Western Texas College in Snyder. He still teaches physical education and health courses there today.

The soldier on the far right in the photograph above (at the Swords of Qadissiya monument, or "Hands of Victory," in Iraq) is Clifford Fargason, who served in the Army from 1972 to 2003 and then as an advisor in Iraq from 2006 to 2007. His father, Hugh Fargason, was a member of Company G and a veteran of World War II. The Fargason family is from the town of Hamleigh. Clifford's son Joshua served in Afghanistan along with First Lieutenant Patrick Jones of Snyder. The Fargasons are also related to Scurry County veteran John Hodnett, who served in World War I.

First Lieutenant Patrick Jones of Snyder, HHTT 4-4 Calvary, 1st Infantry Division, is pictured in Afghanistan on November 7, 2011.

Tommy Doyle was only 15 months old when his father, Jimmie Doyle, left to fight in World War II and never returned. Jimmie was the nose gunner on a B-24 shot down by Japanese antiaircraft fire on September 1, 1944, near the island of Palau. The plane was found by the BentProp Project in January 2004, and the remains of the eight crew members who went down with the plane were recovered in 2008. With Jimmie's remains, they also found his wife's wedding ring. Pictured in March 2005 from left to right are Reid Joyce (member of the BentProp Project), Joe Maldegesang (master diver and Palauan guide), Nancy Doyle (wife of Tommy Doyle), Surangel Whipps (president of the Senate of Palau), Tommy Doyle, and Dr. Pat Scannon (founder of the BentProp Project).

Fletcher Smith and members of the American Legion salute as World War II veteran Nelson Dressler raises the American flag on Veteran's Day 2010 at the nursing home where he is a resident.

Seven

BOOMTOWN

West Texas has long been famous for oil production. Even before petroleum products became as widespread and essential as they are today, entrepreneurs were exploring Scurry County's potential oil resources. This image shows the J.J. Moore No. 1 Well. Located in Ira, it began production on January 27, 1924. It was drilled from February to October 1923, by E.I. (Tommy) Thompson, W.W. Lechner, and E.E. (Buddy) Fogelson of Loutex Corp. W.A. Reiter located the well. Leon English was the field geologist. Drillers were Jesse Thomas, Begossa Murphy, Tom Mann, Charlie Dodson, and Sim Taylor. The tool dresser, James O. Jarmon, was the only man working the well from top to bottom. Pat and Mike Moore, the sons of the landowner, helped to fire the steam roller. The drill struck a pressurized reservoir of cold air (nitrogen and helium), unique in Texas at the time. It blew mud and water 60 feet above the well head. Soon harnessed, it replaced steam to operate the drilling. Completed to 3,575 feet and plugged back to 1,800 feet in the San Andres formation, the J.J. Moore No. 1 yielded over 500,000 barrels of oil. It was the first producing well in Scurry County but would not be the last. In 1948, four widely dispersed wells penetrated the Canyon Reef Formation at depth of 6,500 feet. Soon, more than 2,000 wells defined gigantic fields which contained an estimated four billion barrels of oil. This rapid drilling involved thousands of people: contractors, drillers, engineers, geologists, lawyers, office workers, roughnecks, roustabouts, suppliers. Oil companies poured $300 million into the operations. By 1973, more than 1 billion barrels of oil had been produced. The oil boom placed Snyder on the map, which is where it had always wanted to be. With the sudden influx of residents, the city could not hope to keep up with housing and utilities. Tent communities sprang up everywhere, lines at the bank stretched all the way down the street, and overflow school classes were held in the basement of a local church. Still, the 1950s were a time of prosperity and excitement in Scurry County as penniless "dirt farmers" struck black gold and became millionaires overnight.

m Ameche In Manhattan Hotel

Magnolia Petroleum Company was one of several early oil businesses prior to the boom. A few local families such as the Moores, the Browns, and Edith McKanna were involved in oil production from very early on. In the 1920s and early 1930s, many people in West Texas still did not have cars and people were only speculating about how petroleum products such as plastics would change the world. Small independent companies such as Magnolia were soon supplanted by the oil giants of Chevron and Sun that we know today.

Movie star Don Ameche is reading the local news while staying at The Manhattan Hotel in Snyder. A popular actor of the 1930s and 1940s, Ameche played D'Artagnan in the 1939 version of *The Three Musketeers*. His long career included television appearances on *The Love Boat*, *Columbo*, and many other popular series. He also appeared in the 1985 movie *Cocoon*.

Petroleum pioneer Edith McKanna stands with her car and her airplane. When McKanna was a child, her family moved to Fluvanna where they had held ranching interests since 1880. She was college educated and married James Everett McKanna, who helped to develop the Sharon Ridge oilfield in the early 1920s. James McKanna died in 1932, and Edith McKanna continued to run the business that her husband had started. She became the first woman in Texas to receive a pilot's license and to own her own plane. During her flying career she logged well over 3,000 flying hours. She became a charter member of the 99 Club, composed of the first 99 women pilots in America. During World War II, she donated her plane to the war effort.

In 1945, Edith McKanna organized the Imperial Oil Company and began securing leases. When her discovery well, the Ossie Buffalo, blew in on the Fuller field, Edith McKanna became the only woman oil operator in the Canyon Reef. By 1949, she controlled 86,000 acres and seven producing wells. This photograph shows one of Edith McKanna's oil wells in 1950.

Men are pictured working on a Parkersburg cable-type oil rig. In the early days, what is now done by machinery was mostly accomplished by manpower. These kinds of rigs began producing oil in the 1890s and were used until the 1920s in some areas. This photograph probably dates from around 1925 to 1928.

A drunken man is pictured sleeping under a railroad bridge. Though Scurry County was still a dry county in 1949, the kinds of men attracted by oilfield work were not always law abiding or well behaved.

A house is brought into Snyder on the back of a truck. Housing during the oil boom was a serious issue. Many newcomers lived out of their cars or in tents until they could make enough money to afford to buy a house. Construction crews could not keep up with the demand either, so some folks invested in trailers or prefabricated houses such as this one. Building a house and moving it to the desired site was still a new business in the 1950s, and many locals probably marveled at this residence as it rolled to its destination.

Bill Davidson Sr. shows off a shiny 1954 DeSoto at Davidson Motor Company, which was located near the Phillips 66 on what is now Coliseum Drive in Snyder.

Movie star Bob Hope arrives in Snyder by airplane in this photograph. He owned oil claims in the area and visited often during the boom.

Bob Hope is seen meeting with oilfield workers, who are all clearly excited to be posing with a celebrity.

C.T. McLaughlin, Capt. Eddie Rickenbacker, and Lee Stinson are seen here. Rickenbacker was a famous World War II fighter ace and Medal of Honor recipient, a race car driver, an automotive designer, and a pioneer in air transportation. Stinson was a local pharmacist who also served in World War I. McLaughlin's Diamond M ranch yielded a tremendous amount of oil that helped him to make his fortune. In his later years, he used his money to fund historic preservation and the arts. His large collection of Western Art was exhibited in his "Diamond M" Museum in Snyder for many years. It has since been moved to Texas Tech.

C.T. McLaughlin, Gov. Ray Turner of Oklahoma, and then state senator Lyndon Johnson (arguably McLaughlin's most famous friend) are pictured in 1952 at an oil celebration.

A historical marker commemorates Scurry County's billionth barrel of oil at the site of this pump jack on the side of the highway.

This was the crew of Jessie Brown Well No. 1, one of the early producing wells in Scurry County. On the left is driver I.W. Davis.

Sele Hernandez, Joe Neal Smallwood (owner), and Lanny Lee pose outside of the Phillips 66 station in Snyder. Gas stations sprang up all over town during the boom since many visitors were arriving daily from all over the country, looking for work or trying to stake a claim.

A girl marvels at an ice cream soda poured for her at Dunn's Confectionary. For many people, the 1950s remain synonymous with carhops and soda shops. (Courtesy of the Del Hirst Collection.)

In this c. 1938 photograph is the E&H Cafe in Snyder. Small family restaurants such as this one were overwhelmed during the oil boom with more hungry workers than they could feed during lunch hour. Worley Early, one of the owners, got involved in local politics and ultimately, the restaurant closed. The waitress standing on the right is Gladys Kite who married John Oliver "Ollie" Stimson. Clark Wayne Hudnell, the cook in this photograph, was co-owner of the E&H.

Dr. Johnson reads the newspaper at a local cafe in Scurry County. He brought one of the first cars into Scurry County. One local resident recalls that the Coca-Cola cooler behind him was always filled with lots of ice and soda pop but cannot seem to remember the name of the café where Dr. Johnson is sitting. Many businesses changed hands during the boom, passing from one owner to another whenever someone "struck it rich" in the oil business.

Deep Creek was always prone to flooding. In 1937, a flood did more than $500,000 worth of damages and during the boom years, floods were even more devastating because so many oilfield workers were living out of their cars, in tents, or in poorly constructed housing. Sanitation, usually a challenge, was even more difficult to maintain when the sewers burst thanks to flooding. This photograph was taken in June 1952, and shows a man in a rowboat on Twenty-fifth Street.

Many roads in Scurry County were not yet paved when the oil boom struck. With the increase of traffic, the roads were often muddy after heavy rains.

The oilfield had its share of troubles too, as seen in this photograph of a 1950 fire captured by Joe Dave Scott.

This enormous blaze destroyed the Fuller Cotton Oil Mill in southeast Snyder on November 16, 1942. Cotton oil is extremely flammable and can be much more devastating than an oilfield fire. The land that the cotton mill had stood on was sold off to provide housing for black families, creating what was referred to as "the colored addition" of Snyder. Many of the neighborhood's first residents were former employees of the mill.

Oilfield workers Lloyd Angel (driller), Bob Smith (backup tongs), and Mickey Gonzales (derrick hand) are working on a well.

A celebration in honor of the one-billionth barrel of oil drawn from the Canyon Reef is seen here. Unfortunately, the men in this photograph are not identified, but the Scurry County Museum would very much like to know who they are.

The face of Snyder had changed dramatically with the oil boom, and it became necessary for the courthouse to begin renovations to support the growing community. In this photograph, a man watches from the balcony of the Boren Building as trees are removed from the courthouse lawn. More parking was a necessity, and the space once used for picnics was put to this purpose.

Through the years, the picturesque dome, which had always leaked, became a haven for birds and bats. It was struck by lightning more than once. Finally, when part of the dome fell in, it was removed in 1950.

Eight

SPARKLE CITY

The 1949 boom caused Snyder, population 4,000, to gain more than 7,000 new residents. Jay Rogers, who owned a store in Snyder, started the year with $12,000 in inventory and wound up doing more than $150,000 in business. But it was clear from the beginning that such prosperity could not last forever, and when oil production began to wane, many residents departed for greener pastures. By 1960, the boom had officially gone bust and left behind "a legacy of junk" including poorly constructed houses, broken-down cars, and mountains of trash. Inspired by a contest in *Look* magazine, the city banded together to make improvements. The chamber of commerce organized 19 local clubs and more than 700 citizens to clean up Snyder. They hauled away 5,000 truckloads of debris, including 314 junked cars. They also tore down more than 200 dilapidated buildings and gave a facelift and a new coat of paint to 75 others. All of the rejuvenation brought in more than $10,000 in citizen contributions to be used for attracting new industry. The city also raised $1.25 million in order to build the Scurry County Coliseum. The hard work ultimately paid off, with Snyder winning the title of "All-American Sparkle City" in 1969. In this photograph, workers tear down the facade of a building on the square.

The city council in the 1960s included, from left to right, Bobby McCormick, Marshall Erwin, Bill Johnson, John Hamblen, Jack Lawrence, and Guy Sullivan.

Snyder was awarded the title of "Sparkle City" as part of a contest sponsored by *Look* magazine.

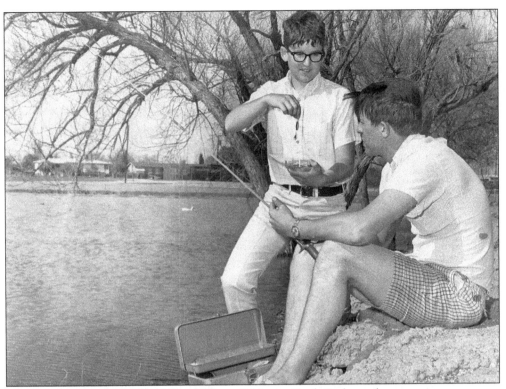

Mark Hargrove (standing) and Kim Hall are fishing at Towle Park pond.

Girls proudly hold up the six historic flags of Texas while riding in the annual Fourth of July parade. This event still draws crowds from all over Scurry County, even when temperatures skyrocket over 100 degrees. The parade formerly circled the Snyder Square but is now held at Towle Park.

Mickey Nunnely, Herb Reed, and city manager George Patterson raise the "All-America City" flag that Snyder received as a result of winning the Sparkle City competition.

This is the official plaque placed on the square to commemorate Sparkle City.

Law enforcement officers gather for a photograph. The police department was first established in Snyder in 1954. As part of the Sparkle City project, money was allotted to outfit police, sheriff's deputies, the fire department, and other city services with the most up to date equipment, including new vehicles and riot gear.

The law enforcement officers of Scurry County had no shortage of opportunities to use their new equipment. A professional thief peeled this safe in the office of Von Roeder Cotton early in the 1960s. Keith Collier, who was sheriff in Scurry County for 32 years, is conducting the investigation.

Snyder wanted to be in the running as a location for Texas Tech way back in 1908. Unfortunately, so did Hermleigh and a number of other communities in Scurry County. Divided, they were conquered, and ultimately the school was built in Lubbock, Texas.

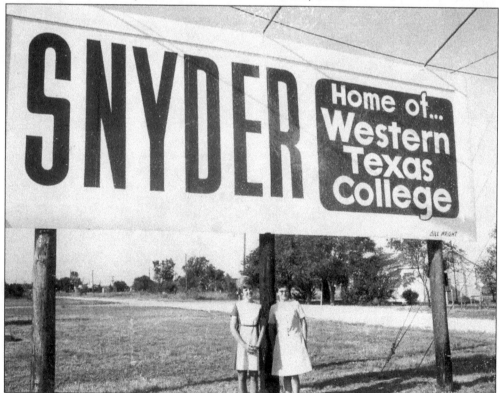

Despite losing out on their bid for Texas Tech, citizens of Scurry County did not give up on their crusade to have a college established close to home. In 1971, after 55 years of community effort, Western Texas College was established in Snyder.

Board members of Western Texas College break ground for construction to begin. Pictured from left to right are R.C. Patton, Bill Wilson Jr., Bill Jones, M.L. Broman, Robert Hargrove, George Patterson, Edwin Parks, and Dr. Robert Clinton, the first WTC president.

The original faculty of WTC is seen here. As Jerry Baird describes, Western Texas College originally set out to be different from other colleges by not competing for the highest achieving students, but instead offering an education to those who were most in need. "We only had one building at the time," Baird recalls "But (when the college opened) we had more than 600 people show up." For a town the size of Snyder, that was quite the turnout. The first class was composed of a wide variety of students including high school seniors trying to get ahead and retirees eager to learn something new. Today, WTC has students from many countries, including Brazil, Jamaica, and Nigeria.

Western Texas College is pictured from above.

The Scurry County Museum was built during the second phase of WTC construction when several local organizations with a common interest in history banded together. Pictured are Ernest Sears, Harriet "Hootie" Redwine, Paula Lunsford, and an unidentified woman. Two of the individuals in this photograph, Carol Cramer Bullard (second from right) and Drew Bullard (far right), are still affiliated with the museum today.

Western Texas College has long been proud of its student athletes. In 1979 and 1980, coach Nolan Richardson, who went on to coach the University of Arkansas in the Final Four, led the WTC Westerners to NJCAA victory in basketball. In 1994, with Richardson at the helm, Arkansas won the national championship. Richardson remains the only coach to win all three collegiate championships, ranging from NJCAA to NIT and NCAA.

Members of the 1979–1980 team include, from left to right, Ronald Partee, Freddie Davis, Keith Dennis, Oscar Alvarado, David Brown, James Hutchinson, Jim Price, Greg Stewart, Donald Warren, Paul Pressey (who went on to play in the NBA), Bill Patterson, Phil Spradling (who went on to coach at WTC), Dewan Vantrey, Franklin Bennett, and Joey Rozales; (kneeling) Coach Richardson and an unidentified trainer.

Those who proclaimed, "I'm In!" supported the establishment of the Price Daniel Unit in Scurry County. Bringing a prison to Scurry County was a controversial move, and many of those who were financially secure protested that doing so would lower property values and cause crime to increase in Snyder. When supporters of the prison faced criticism that they were "poor and ignorant," they responded by adopting that phrase as a rallying call. The Price Daniel Unit created many desperately needed jobs in Scurry County. From left to right are Shaun Ragland, Dab Johnson, and an unidentified man.

The Price Daniel Unit is pictured as it looks today, surrounded by wind turbines and cotton fields.

Nine

WILD WEST TEXAS

Who says the Wild West is dead? For a deeply religious, dry, and nominally law-abiding region, Scurry County certainly has had its share of colorful characters. Some photographs simply defy all explanation but are sure to inspire a good laugh. The folks in this 1916 photograph are getting some good ol' fashioned exercise, or at least that is what we think they are doing. Pictured are Wade and Charlie Winston and the Newton family on a fishing trip to the Double Fork of the Brazos.

Scurry County was dry until 2004, but during the oil boom no one seemed to really comprehend what that meant. Law enforcement regularly caught moonshiners and bootleggers. In this photograph, Sheriff Frank Brownfield and Deputy Horace Leath stand beside a still, which they found in Knapp. One local bootlegger, Son Davis, claimed that he started selling liquor illegally when he was only nine years old.

The girl on the left in this photograph looks smart in a very tomboyish black bowler hat. The same cannot be said for the man seated in front of her, who seems to be wearing her bonnet. Photographed are Ida Mellard, Albert Tinker, and Edna Tinker around 1910. What were they thinking? No one will ever guess.

Rapunzel, Rapunzel, let down your hair! This unidentified girl, photographed in 1914, had some serious long locks to contend with. Imagine brushing hair like that after a long day out in the West Texas wind!

A member of the Faver family takes a washtub bath on the porch of his house. Many parts of Scurry County did not have electricity until the late 1940s or 1950s. Old-timers fondly recall how families "made do" in the days before indoor plumbing. More than a few claim that they were always "the last one in the bath." This man better have been the last to wash in his family. It sure does not look like there is very much water left!

In a blue-collar town full of cowboys and roughnecks, a man's wardrobe usually consists of one or two pairs of jeans, a felt hat for winter and a straw hat for summer. In Scurry County, men are men—except when there is fundraising to be done. Look closely at this bridal portrait, which was made around 1900. There is not a single woman in the wedding party, and that includes the bride!

This spring style show was assembled by the American Legion auxiliary in December 1929. Members of the "Womanless Style Show" include Jesse Jones, Hadley Reeve, Ross Pate, Tollie Faver, Roy Davis, Joe Brown, Emmitt Butts, Earl Strawn, Joe Wilson, Jim Norred, Tommie Todd, A.W. Yeats, Hal Latimore, J.D. Pigman, and Elmer Louder, who apparently ran off before anyone could photograph him wearing his old lady's knickers.

Seen here is a rabbit drive in Hermleigh. Rabbits were so numerous that boys and men (and sometimes a few tough young girls) would gather and hunt as many of them as they could. If they were not exterminated, rabbits could cost a farming family their livelihood.

Snuffer scalps 1,000 rabbits! Though the Mooar brothers killed an estimated 22,000 buffalo, Snyder's John Snuffer set his sights a little lower. During the Depression, when rabbits were decimating crops, he achieved local fame by hunting 1,000 of them.

The monster rattlesnake above must have helped itself to more than a few rabbits. Rattlesnakes are a persistent problem in West Texas. The nearby city of Sweetwater in Nolan County has hosted the World's Largest Rattlesnake Roundup since 1958. Thousands of western diamondback rattlesnakes are captured, measured, beheaded, skinned, deep-fried, and eaten during this annual event. Scurry County ranchers are usually happy to supply some to the Sweetwater Jaycees who run the roundup. The tree in the image below is full of rattlesnakes.

No snow for a dogsled here in Snyder! It is a good thing that Bill Brown has his wolf and dog team hooked up to a buggy in this photograph. He departed from Nome, Alaska, on May 5, 1912, bound for Washington DC. This photograph was possibly taken on August 7, 1913.

A boy feeds a treat to a visiting circus elephant on Avenue R. around 1950.

Who let the baby drive? With much work always needing to be done on a farm, children were often expected to entertain themselves. Of course, that did not include taking the family car for a drive! One old-timer, however, recalls being put up on phone books so that he could drive his father's truck into town. His father would send him out to purchase cigarettes for him when he was only 12 years old!

It seems that nobody told the folks in this photograph that fishing usually involves rods, fishing line, and sometimes even a boat. From the looks of things, the fish were not biting on this fishing trip, but the men did catch themselves a mighty fine log. Pictured here are Mr. and Mrs. H.G. Towle, Mr. and Mrs. Joe Caton, Mr. and Mrs. Jim Lockhart, County Judge and Mrs. Adamson, Mr. and Mrs. W.C. Fullilove, Mr. and Mrs. J.W. Couch, and children of the families.

Charlie Lockhart came to Snyder in 1898. He ran for county treasurer in 1900 and roomed in his office until he could find a better place to live. He was reelected eight times and in 1930, he became state treasurer. *Ripley's Believe It or Not* ran an article on Lockart, proclaiming that, "the biggest state in the Union has the smallest state treasurer, only 45 inches tall!" Lockhart himself did not believe that he was hindered by his size. He stated simply that he was "a little man with big ideas."

Charlie Lockhart was not the only extremely short citizen of Scurry County to establish a supersize reputation. Jimmie Billingsley (pistol) was a district clerk in Scurry County and held other offices as well. Along with Brud Boren (pitchfork) and Al Simpson (rifle) in this 1941 photograph, he poses to send a message to anyone looking to make trouble in Snyder—Judge Pinto Bean will uphold the law! According to those who knew him, Jimmie Billingsley was a smart and well-loved man who enjoyed making people laugh.

Epilogue

THEN AND NOW

When was this photograph taken? At first glance, it is easy to mistake this July 4, 1996, photograph for an image of yesteryear. Only the telephone lines in the background and the shorts and T-shirts of parade watchers give the whole story away. Texas is a state proud of its own heritage, and Scurry County is no exception. Traditions established more than a century ago persist today. A number of Snyder civic clubs can trace their origins back to the beginning of the 20th century, and many local ranching families can tell you where their ancestors built their first "dugout" homes.

Beverly Sims was the daughter of Gladys Johnson and Ed Sims. This photograph was taken around 1928. Beverly was very young when her mother shot her father on the Snyder Square in 1916. When the gunfire began, she was grabbed from the car and carried into her grandfather's bank.

Beverly Benson (Sims), author Bill O'Neal, and Scurry County Museum director Daniel Schlegel Jr. are photographed at the Snyder book signing of Bill O'Neal's book *The Johnson-Sims Feud: Romeo and Juliet West Texas Style*. The signing was held on December 16, 2011, on the anniversary of the shooting which ignited the feud. Beverly attended the presentation. Despite the hardship that the feud caused for her family, she was proud to be a part of Scurry County history. She fondly recalled Texas Ranger Frank Hamer, describing her stepfather as one of the finest men she had ever known. Beverly Benson passed away shortly after the event.

Members of the Kiwanis Club are seen here making pancakes in 1951.

The Kiwanis are still making pancakes in 2012. Pictured from left to right are Wendell Ferguson, Daniel Schlegel Jr., Trey Wilson, Phyllis Dominguez, and Linda Hughes.

This November 1934 photograph is of the Altrurian Club Love Feast. Pictured are Mrs. Hamilton, Mrs. Pat Brown, Mrs. Lee Stinson, Mrs. Jack Harris, Mrs. Carl Yoder, Florence Leftwich, Mrs. R.D. English, Mrs. Curnutte, Mrs. Higgin Waddill, Mrs. Preuitt, Mrs. Roland Bell, Mrs. Andy Anderson, Mrs. Jake Smythe, Mrs. H.H. Towle, Mrs. Joe Stinson, Mrs. O.P. Thrane, Nancy Caton, and Mrs. Fred Grayum. The club was established in 1908.

This photograph shows members of the Altrurian Club today. Pictured from left to right are (first row) Carolyn Martin, Mary Murff, Ann Cross, Mary Ann Key, Wyvone Davis, and Dora Blakey; (second row) Francene Noah, Beverly Robertson, Maria Patterson, Janelle Hammack, Kay Echols, Jackie McNew, Bobbie Lockhart, Bobbie Taylor, Vera Falls, and Joyce Fuqua. Not pictured are members D'Ann Grimmett, Kay Hensley, JoAnn Littlepage, and Nina Nesbit.

The chamber of commerce is seen in this 1920 photograph. From left to right are (first row) Andy Anderson, Pete Thrane, Ralph Odom, D.P. Yoder, H.P. Wellborn, H.J. Brice, Bob Warren, Joe Stinson, and Bill Jones; (second row) Gay McGlaun, unidentified, Homer Jenkins, Roy Hendricks, Ray Strayhorn, Frank Brownfield, Pat Bullock, Lee Grant, Judge Holley, Horace Leath, J.L. Martin, and unidentified.

Members of the board of directors for the Snyder Chamber of Commerce in 2012 are seen here. Pictured from left to right are Sandra Salinas, Melissa Elam, Janell Jones, Billy Mebane, Roy Bartels, Robbi Tindol, David Nazier, Janet Spence, Merle Taylor, Bill Crist, Tim McCullar, and Bill Robertson.

Lake J.B. Thomas, a Colorado River Municipal Water District project, is pictured soon after its completion in the early 1970s.

Today, Lake J.B. Thomas is virtually empty. In the arid region of West Texas, water can be a scarce commodity. The importance of conserving this resource is often not realized until a drought or a wildfire strikes. These days, Deep Creek rarely lives up to its name. When spring rains got the water flowing in 2012, several Snyder residents were so excited that they went to take photographs.

The 1911 Scurry County Courthouse was renovated first in the 1950s and then again in 1972. A granite shell was constructed around the original building. Columns and windows can still be seen inside storage closets on the third floor. The style of architecture is Brutalism. The courthouse was designed by J.D. Hinton and is considered to be one of the best examples of this architectural style.

This is the Scurry County Courthouse as it appears today.

The Roscoe, Snyder & Pacific Railroad stopped carrying passengers in 1953, and most of its tracks have not been used since 1984.

Two historic train depots still stand in Snyder, though trains no longer carry passengers through Scurry County. The former Santa Fe depot designed by Louis Curtiss was listed as one of Preservation Texas's "Most Endangered Historic Places" in 2011. The depot is vacant and boarded up.

Some sports, such as football, baseball, and tennis, have been popular in Scurry County since the 1920s.

The Korean martial art of Tae Kwon Do came to Snyder in the 1970s. Master Greg Gafford's West Texas Tae Kwo Do school has hosted tournaments and campouts for 26 years.

In 2011, writer/director Tanner Beard, a graduate of Snyder High School, produced a feature-length film titled *The Legend of Hell's Gate* with a number of Snyder actors as well as a few Hollywood veterans.

In this scene, Buck Taylor (of *Gunsmoke* fame) plays Pete Snyder, who is exhibiting the hide of the white buffalo outside of his store. Also pictured are Snyder actor Kevin Alejandro, who has appeared on the television show *True Blood*, and Jim Beaver playing J. Wright Mooar.

This is the hide of the white buffalo shot by J. Wright Mooar in 1876, on display in the home of Judy Hays. Our story ends where it began, with the buffalo.

Visit us at
arcadiapublishing.com

Printed in the USA
CPSIA information can be obtained
at www.ICGtesting.com
LVHW071459041223
765647LV00008B/151